God's Dream Team

"Jesus Created You For Greatness"

By

Evangelist Ivory & Phyllis Herd

God's Dream Team

"Jesus Created You For Greatness"

By:

Evangelist Ivory & Phyllis Herd

Copyright@2014
All Rights Reserved, Printed in The USA

Published By:

ABM Publications
A division of Andrew Bills Ministries, Inc.
PO Box 6811, Orange, CA 92863
www.abmpublications.com

ISBN: 978-1-931820-26-4

All scripture quotations, unless otherwise indicated are taken from The Holy Bible, King James Version 1977, Thomas Nelson Publishing, The New American Standard Bible 2003, the New King James Version 1977, Thomas Nelson Publishing and the New International Version 1984. International Bible Society. They are used by permission, with all rights reserved.

TABLE OF CONTENTS

	Acknowledgments	1
	Introduction	3
1	Jesus Gave Us The Vision	5
2	God's Dream Team	9
3	Foundational Vision Of Kings & Queens	21
4	Overseeing Your Vision	25
5	God's Team Order	35
	Notes	41
	Ministry Contact Information	45

ACKNOWLEDGEMENTS

- I would like to give Thanks and Honor to My Wife (Phyllis)- Co Author of The Vision of Our Lord. It is written when a Man find's a Wife he finds a good thing. Also I'm first to admit, I found a Virtuous Woman, a True Helpmate that was Created for me. This Holy Spirit Message from Haven, Our Lord Jesus wants to see his Dream Team Restored. I have to say Baby, "You are the Best, A True Wife and Servant."

- Our Beloved Bishops Levoid and Marie Trimble, who always are imparting the Lord's Spirit and Words to us. Thank You for being our Loving Shepherds. Our Church **-Resurrection Life Center 3655 Fernwood Ave, Lynwood, CA.**

- To our Spiritual Father and Mother, Prelate-Bishop Napoleon and Mother Ruth Rhoades of the Convention of Covenanting Churches Org. (CCC). For They Married Us and They have Counseled us all these years. We Love You Both! **(website: 3csministries.com)**

- To Our Brother: Minister of Music- Johnny Williams and His Wife, Evangelist Joycelyn Williams (Our Anointed Sister-in-Law) of Joycelyn Williams Ministries, who continue to go forward in the Vision of Building up the Body of Christ by holding Dynamic Conferences for the Lord's Body. We Love You!

(website at: positioned2beblessed.com)

- To our Brother and Sister in Christ: Pastor Andrew and First Lady Ann Marie Bills. Thank You for Your Encouragement and Help with This Publication. You are always showing Your Love, by Your Service to Others. You are a Blessing from God. We Love You! **(website at: andrewbills.com)**

INTRODUCTION

Jesus Gave Us The Vision For Victory In Our Relationship.

As We look at some of the Fruit of our Relationships We find Ourselves sometimes Discouraged or Broken at times, even Mad! We know in our Hearts that our Fruit is not as Sweet and Full of Life as it should be. Our Lord Jesus said. "He is the Vine and We are the Branches", it is His Will to Produce Heavenly Fruit. John (15:5) It is Written that God's Thoughts are not Mans'. (i.e. the worlds') His thoughts are Higher Than Man's. Isaiah (55: 8-9)

The Holy Spirit is showing us how to Abide in Jesus (i.e. sit in the middle of God's sweet fruit, producing Power.) Some might say "I'm not going to do that." But look at the word of God in this Book, this is Evidence that his way works because HE ORDERED IT, AND STANDS WITH IT WITH HIS LIFE GIVING POWER!!!

LET US BEGIN!

EVANGELIST IVORY & PHYLLIS HERD

CHAPTER 1

Jesus Gave Us The Vision

Our Lord Jesus, who is our Heavenly Bride Groom, is soon coming for his Bride who he Loves. But until then, his bride must show her love by being in subjection to his Lordship, as his Beloved. This is the Lord's pattern for Order, which should help with Unity, bringing anointing and empowering Love and Victory for our Family.

From the Book of (1 Peter)- Apostle Paul said Peter(Cephas), had his wife with him in ministry. (1 Corinthians (9:5), also the other team that helped Paul many times, when there was no one else, was Husband and Wife Team –<u>Aquila (eagle)</u> and <u>Priscilla (ancient),</u> they were fellow workers). (Romans (16:3)

I have ministered to many Men and Women. My Job in the Hospital has over 300 women. God has brought to my attention mostly, all the positions of Leadership on my job, women are holding. So when I see men employees, coming to do a job of service or installing something, some women give orders and some ask in the spirit of Abigail, which <u>influenced</u> David. Men can't help but to bend over backward to help the Women. Even in the world few Women use their <u>influence.</u> When a Godly King knows his Queen is submitted and holds him in reverence, he will esteem her impute, help, gifts, abilities and influence. I believe like the Queen, who is the **(Proverb 31)** ***Virtuous Women and Her King Lemuel.***

The Lord told me, Women are smarter than Men in the everyday multiple tasks of life. But only God can Lead a Family. Most Women believe they are smarter than their Man. They say men can only do one thing at a time. Leadership is based on one thing;   **Hearing, Doing and Abiding in Jesus.**

When Godly Men find themselves in a lot of things, that are or aren't gifted, in or new or above their level of wisdom, we ask Jesus a lot in single mindness.

A Godly Man in his weakness and inabilities must come to Jesus for Leadership. Even at our best only **JESUS KNOWS, WHY, WHAT, WHEN AND WHERE TO MOVE UPON THE FAMILY VISION. (Proverbs 3:5-6)** [5] Trust in the LORD with all thine heart; and lean not unto thine own understanding. ⁶ In all thy ways acknowledge him, and he shall direct thy paths.

1 Peter 3:1-12

3 Likewise, ye wives, be in subjection to your own husbands; that, if any obey not the word, they also may without the word be won by the conversation of the wives;

² While they behold your chaste conversation coupled with fear.

³ Whose adorning let it not be that outward adorning of plaiting the hair, and of wearing of gold, or of putting on of apparel;

⁴ But let it be the hidden man of the heart, in that which is not corruptible, even the ornament of a meek and quiet spirit, which is in the sight of God of great price.

⁵ For after this manner in the old time the holy women also, who trusted in God, adorned themselves, being in subjection unto their own husbands:

⁶ Even as Sara obeyed Abraham, calling him lord: whose daughters ye are, as long as ye do well, and are not afraid with any amazement.

⁷ Likewise, ye husbands, dwell with them according to knowledge, giving honour unto the wife, as unto the weaker vessel, and as being heirs together of the grace of life; that your prayers be not hindered.

⁸ Finally, be ye all of one mind, having compassion one of another, love as brethren, be pitiful, be courteous:

⁹ Not rendering evil for evil, or railing for railing: but contrariwise blessing; knowing that ye are thereunto called, that ye should inherit a blessing.

¹⁰ For he that will love life, and see good days, let him refrain his tongue from evil, and his lips that they speak no guile:

¹¹ Let him eschew evil, and do good; let him seek peace, and ensue it.

¹² For the eyes of the Lord are over the righteous, and his ears are open unto their prayers: but the face of the Lord is against them that do evil.

CHAPTER 2

GOD'S DREAM TEAM

- God's Dream Team started with Adam and Eve.
- <u>Man's</u> Place is Leadership
- <u>Woman,</u> with Help and Influence, to bring God's Vision of Mankind into Fullness.

<u>Some Examples of God's Dream Team are as follows:</u>

1. ADAM AND EVE

Genesis 2: (7-9) ⁷And the L<small>ORD</small> God formed man of the dust of the ground, and breathed into his nostrils the breath of life; and man became a living soul.

⁸ And the L<small>ORD</small> God planted a garden eastward in Eden; and there he put the man whom he had formed.

⁹ And out of the ground made the L<small>ORD</small> God to grow every tree that is <u>**pleasant**</u> to the sight, and <u>good</u> for food; **<u>the tree of life</u>** also in the midst of

the garden, and the **tree of knowledge** of **good** and **evil.**

Genesis 2: (15-19)

¹⁵ And the LORD God took the man, and put him into the garden of Eden to **dress** * (5647c)-to serve as husband man-worshipper) it and to **keep** *(8104c)- to guard and keep watch) it.

¹⁶ And the LORD God <u>commanded</u> the man, saying, Of every tree of the garden thou mayest freely eat:

¹⁷ But of the tree of the knowledge of **good** and **evil,** thou shalt not eat of it: for in the day that thou eatest thereof thou shalt surely <u>die.</u>

¹⁸ And the LORD God said, It is not good that the man should be alone; I will make him an **help (one who helps)** meet(mate) for him.

¹⁹ And out of the ground the LORD God formed every beast of the field, and every fowl of the air; and brought them unto Adam to see what he would <u>call them</u>: and whatsoever Adam called every living creature, that was the name thereof.

Genesis 2: (21-24)

²¹ And the LORD God caused a deep sleep to fall upon Adam, and he slept: and he took one of his ribs, and closed up the flesh instead thereof;

²² And the rib, which the LORD God had taken from man, made he a woman, and brought her unto the man.

²³ And Adam said, This is now bone of my bones, and flesh of my flesh: she shall be called Woman, because she was taken out of Man.

²⁴ Therefore shall a man leave his father and his mother, and shall **cleave** *-(fast together) (1692c) unto his wife: and they shall be one flesh. **Genesis 3: (1-6) Overview- Serpent Bequiled woman-she gave unto her husband the forbidden fruit. <u>(She could influence her husband.)</u>**

Genesis 3:(12-17)

¹² And the man said, The woman whom thou gavest to be with me, she gave me of the tree, and I did eat.

¹³ And the LORD God said unto the woman, What is this that thou hast done? And the woman said, The serpent beguiled me, and I did eat.

¹⁴ And the LORD God said <u>unto</u> the serpent, Because thou hast done this, thou art cursed above all cattle, and above every beast of the field; upon thy belly shalt thou go, and dust shalt thou eat all the days of thy life:

¹⁵ And I will put enmity between thee and the woman, and between thy seed and her seed; it shall bruise thy head, and thou shalt bruise his heel.

¹⁶ Unto the woman he said, I will greatly multiply thy sorrow and thy conception; in sorrow thou shalt bring forth children; and thy ***desire*** shall be to thy husband, and he shall ***rule*** over thee.

¹⁷ And unto Adam he said, Because thou hast **hearkened** unto the voice of thy wife **(she could influence** her husband**)** and hast eaten of the tree, of which I commanded thee, saying, Thou shalt not eat of it: cursed is the ground for thy sake; in sorrow shalt thou eat **of** it all the days of thy life;

2. Noah and Wife

Note of Interest: Adam and Noah, 10 generations. Nine of them lived over 900 years, their lives overlapped each other. Adam died 126 years before Noah was born. **Genesis 6: (7-8)** And the LORD said, I will destroy man whom I have created from the face of the earth; both man, and beast, and the creeping thing, and the fowls of the air; for it repenteth me that I have made them. ⁸But Noah found <u>grace</u> in the eyes of the LORD.

3. Abraham and Sarah

Note of Interest: Noah died 2 years before Abraham was born. Noah son <u>Shem</u> was one of the forefather's of Abraham. Abraham's wife was his half sister, same Father. **Genesis 12:(1-2) (1)** God calls Abram-Lord said Abram, get thee out of thy country and from thy kindred, and from thy Father's house. Unto a land that I will show thee; ²And I will make of thee a great nation, and I will bless thee, and make thy name great; and thou covenant with Abram shalt be a blessing:

Genesis 14: (17) Note of Interest: Melchizedek Blesses him. In **Genesis 15:(1)** The Lord came unto Abram in a vision, saying, fear not, Abram: I am thy shield, and the exceeding great reward. In **Genesis 15:(1-17)** The Lord makes a Covenant with Abram to tell him about the future of his seed- Egypt the people of the Promise land even the giants. Genesis 16- Sarai <u>influence</u> Abram to go into Hagar. Genesis 17- God appeared to Abram changes his name to Abraham. Then God told Abraham to call his wife Sarah. Genesis 17:(13) God told Abraham to circumcise his whole house as a sign of covenant between me and you. Even servants and strangers wanted to stay among then. Genesis 17:(19) For I know him, (The Lord said of Abraham) that he will command his children and his household after him, and they shall keep the way of the Lord, to do justice and judgement, that the Lord may bring upon Abraham that which he hath spoken of him.

4. Isaac and Rebekah
(he laughs-03327c) (ensnarer-07259c)

Note of Interest - Abraham's Father Terah had three son's. Abram, Nahor and Haran. Nahor also married his half sister, Mileah-daughter of Haran, Genesis 11:(29)). Also Lot was the Son of Haran, Genesis 11:(31)- Rebekah was Lot's Sister, Genesis 24:(24) The Family had the Vision from Noah-Abraham. Abraham sent his servant back to his Kindred for a Wife for his son (he made his servant promise, no Canaanites women). I think even them don't be unequally yoked with unbeliever, 2 Corn: 6:(14). Abraham's servant prayed to Lord God of Heaven for a wife for Abraham's son. Genesis 24: (12-13). In his servants thoughts, he said the one who gives me a drink of water and these 10 camels she's the one for my Master's son. Rebekah name means "ensnarer" (7259c). She was able to be with a Rich Husband!

5. The People of Moab and Midian

From the Book of Numbers: (Chapter22 -25). The Moab was trying to defeat the Israelite's (God's People). The King of the Moabs, (Balak) - he sent for a man who was a wizard, to come and curse them. The wizard tried but God wouldn't let the words come out of his mouth. So the next idea was to use women to make them go against God. The Moabite women Influence them into whoredom and worshiping their Gods'.

Please Note: (Satan will always try to use influence for Dishonor, Discard and Division making God's Team ineffective).

6. David and Abigail

David (Beloved) and Abigail (My Father is Joy i.e.} or source of my Joy) speaks about David watching a rich man name Nabal's, (name means fool) 3,000 sheep and 1,000 goats protecting them from Bandits, who were trying to take them. David's men were starving and they did not take one sheep or goat. When David told his man to tell Nabal how they had been protecting his sheep and goats from Bandits, even Nabal's sheppard said, "because of David they were safe." Nabal said he did not care who David was or that his men risk their lives for his sheep and goats. 1 Samuel 25:(13) David told 400 of his men to arm themselves, because they were going to kill every man in his house. 1 Samuel (25:22) Abigail heard what David was going to do with her Husband (Nabal). In the following Chapter (1 Samuel 25: (23-35) this is the action that she preceded with.

[23] And when Abigail saw David, she hasted, and lighted off the ass, and fell before David on her face, and bowed herself to the ground,

[24] And fell at his feet, and said, Upon me, my lord, upon me let this iniquity be: and let thine

handmaid, I pray thee, speak in thine audience, and hear the words of thine handmaid.

²⁵ Let not my lord, I pray thee, regard this man of Belial, even Nabal: for as his name is, so is he; Nabal is his name, and folly is with him: but I thine handmaid saw not the young men of my lord, whom thou didst send.

²⁶ Now therefore, my lord, as the LORD liveth, and as thy soul liveth, seeing the LORD hath withholden thee from coming to shed blood, and from avenging thyself with thine own hand, now let thine enemies, and they that seek evil to my lord, be as Nabal.

²⁷ And now this blessing which thine handmaid hath brought unto my lord, let it even be given unto the young men that follow my lord.

²⁸ I pray thee, forgive the trespass of thine handmaid: for the LORD will certainly make my lord a sure house; because my lord fighteth the battles of the LORD, and evil hath not been found in thee all thy days.

²⁹ Yet a man is risen to pursue thee, and to seek thy soul: but the soul of my lord shall be bound in the bundle of life with the LORD thy God; and the

souls of thine enemies, them shall he sling out, as out of the middle of a sling.

[30] And it shall come to pass, when the LORD shall have done to my lord according to all the good that he hath spoken concerning thee, and shall have appointed thee ruler over Israel;

[31] That this shall be no grief unto thee, nor offence of heart unto my lord, either that thou hast shed blood causeless, or that my lord hath avenged himself: but when the LORD shall have dealt well with my lord, then remember thine handmaid.

[32] And David said to Abigail, Blessed be the LORD God of Israel, which sent thee this day to meet me:

[33] And blessed be thy advice, and blessed be thou, which hast kept me this day from coming to shed blood, and from avenging myself with mine own hand.

[34] For in very deed, as the LORD God of Israel liveth, which hath kept me back from hurting thee, except thou hadst hasted and come to meet me, surely there had not been left unto Nabal by the morning light any that pisseth against the wall.

³⁵ So David received of her hand that which she had brought him, and said unto her, Go up in peace to thine house; see, I have **hearkened** (influence) to thy voice, and have accepted thy person.

CHAPTER 3

The Foundational Vision of Kings and Queens in Christ

King Lemuel and His Virtuous Queen

Proverbs 31 (KJV)

31 The words of king Lemuel, the prophecy that his mother taught him.

² What, my son? and what, the son of my womb? and what, the son of my vows?

³ Give not thy strength unto women, nor thy ways to that which destroyeth kings.

⁴ It is not for kings, O Lemuel, it is not for kings to drink wine; nor for princes strong drink:

⁵ Lest they drink, and forget the law, and pervert the judgment of any of the afflicted.

⁶ Give strong drink unto him that is ready to perish, and wine unto those that be of heavy hearts.

⁷ Let him drink, and forget his poverty, and remember his misery no more.

⁸ Open thy mouth for the dumb in the cause of all such as are appointed to destruction.

⁹ Open thy mouth, judge righteously, and plead the cause of the poor and needy.

¹⁰ Who can find a virtuous woman? for her price is far above rubies.

¹¹ The heart of her husband doth safely trust in her, so that he shall have no need of spoil.

¹² She will do him good and not evil all the days of her life.

¹³ She seeketh wool, and flax, and worketh willingly with her hands.

¹⁴ She is like the merchants' ships; she bringeth her food from afar.

¹⁵ She riseth also while it is yet night, and giveth meat to her household, and a portion to her maidens.

¹⁶ She considereth a field, and buyeth it: with the fruit of her hands she planteth a vineyard.

17 She girdeth her loins with strength, and strengtheneth her arms.

18 She perceiveth that her merchandise is good: her candle goeth not out by night.

19 She layeth her hands to the spindle, and her hands hold the distaff.

20 She stretcheth out her hand to the poor; yea, she reacheth forth her hands to the needy.

21 She is not afraid of the snow for her household: for all her household are clothed with scarlet.

22 She maketh herself coverings of tapestry; her clothing is silk and purple.

23 Her husband is known in the gates, when he sitteth among the elders of the land.

24 She maketh fine linen, and selleth it; and delivereth girdles unto the merchant.

25 Strength and honour are her clothing; and she shall rejoice in time to come.

26 She openeth her mouth with wisdom; and in her tongue is the law of kindness.

27 She looketh well to the ways of her household,

and eateth not the bread of idleness.

[28] Her children arise up, and call her blessed; her husband also, and he praiseth her.

29 Many daughters have done virtuously, but thou excellest them all.

30 Favour is deceitful, and beauty is vain: but a woman that feareth the Lord, she shall be in the gates.

31 Give her of the fruit of her hands; and let her own works praise her in the gates.

CHAPTER 4

OVERSEENG YOUR VISION

1. The Female Eagle test for a mate by picking a branch and flying up with it, dropping it while all the prospective mates compete to catch it. The male eagle who can, as she takes it higher and dropping the branch can catch it three times will be chosen to be her mate. He is going to need that commitment because Eagle's mate for life. Her mate is going to need those skills to catch the young when teaching them to fly.

    a. Woman of God - to chose your prospective mate (Luke 6:44) The word of Of God says you will know them by their Fruit. There are some tests you must consider: Is the man Saved? Is he filled with the Holy Spirit? Does he know how to worship our Lord Jesus? Does he read his Word" Does his Bible look well used? Does he have a Pray Life? Can he Pray Out Loud? (i.e. The Promises of God)? Is he a Church Member and How Long? Does he have a Job and how long have he been on the job? Was he ever married? Does he have any Children. <u>Now it is time to Pray and Fast to see the Lord's Will on this Union.</u>

2. When the male and female Eagle mate, they mate for Life. They pick a high place in the cliff just like we should in the rock (Jesus) for their nest, the male flies again and again getting branches for the nest.. When he is done, <u>he pluck's out some of his feathers</u> to make the nest soft.(like a Husbands' sacrifice for his family) Then he puts thorns outside the nest for protection. Genesis 2:(15) <u>Adam was told by God to dress- (work) and keep (protect)</u> the garden. (3) Both eagles take turns sitting on their eggs. (4). They both hunt for food and feed the babies after Birth. When it is time to learn to fly, the female takes the feathers out of the nest so the thorns are exposed, then the female pushes them out, one at a time, so they can learn to fly. At the same time the male eagle(Father) circling in the air catching the young eagle on his back, before the young eagle hits the ground. He takes the young eagle to a high

rock and does it over and over until he learns how to flap his wings and flies on his own. Proverbs 22:(6) Train up a child in the way he should go: and when he is old, he will not depart from it. Husbands, the Lord said: "He chose Abraham", because he will command his children and household after him and they shall keep the way of the Lord. Genesis 18:(19).

a. <u>Husbands you are the Leader,</u> (God called you to Lead) 1 Corinthians 11: (13). Just like the Eagle lifting the Family on a high rock, you are called to Lead in the ways of the Lord. (anointing, praying, teaching and praising) Wives you help maintain the atmosphere, i.e.(when observing the Passover Meal (Easter). The women Light the candles' at the start of the meal, this tradition came about because of Eve in the garden, she yielded to Satan or (darkness) and brought it to Adam. Now the Wife is lighting the candle, proclaiming light be restored. (It is written that the seed of the women shall bruise Satan's head: (Jesus). Genesis 3:(15) The spirit of the woman can influence the whole house.

3. Fathers' the Lord call us to speak the Blessing over our Family. Me and My Wife, every morning I go to Work anoint each other with oil and speak the Blessing. i.e.(promises of God for that fruit or ability), because if offence, envying and strife comes in, next is confusion and every evil work will follow. (James 3:16).

4. The Anointing to change our ways and help our inabilities are by the Power of the Holy Spirit Acts 1:(8) When we are submitting ourselves one to another. Ephesians 5:(21) We must do so that our Prayers will be heard and answered. 1Peter 3:(7) If you have children at home, grown or young in the household. Bind and Loose (Matthew 16:19) speaking impartation Blessing (i.e. scriptures- promises)

5. Husbands' like Abraham saying to everyone it's time to go to church. Wife support this, Please. . Everyone up and out the nest you must together teach them how to fly. Husband lead in Thanksgiving, Worship and the Word. Above all Lead in Love!

6. The Eagle flies the highest of any other bird. He soars'(i.e. gliding) not flapping his wings but using and reading the wind even to the point where the eagle can read stormy winds and use the wind's Power to rise above the storm, if self. We must Teach our Children how to walk in the mighty Wind of God.(i.e. Holy Spirit)

a. Eagles have eyes that they can see their prey many miles away. Train our children with Gods' Promises, so they know what Jesus Paid for Them. They will know where their Blessings are Located. (i.e. jobs, mate's, gifts, talents. and where to sow Financial Blessings).

7. The Eagle has lens on their eyes, no other bird can look directly into the sun, but the Eagle can. We have been given charge by our Lord to train up our Children in the way they should go, by our Lord Jesus. Proverbs 22:(6) We must teach them how to Behold Jesus(i.e. look to him) <u>Our Son of God</u> , so they may be changed into his image from Glory to Glory.2 Corinthians 3:(18) Do not make decisions concerning

the children without letting each other know for unity and respect of Family Leadership. Even Adults must maintain God's Order for the Family. If you don't agree with each other never show division in front of children. Go into another room together, discuss it, if there still no agreement; Pray, even fast-to hear from God. If still no agreement then the Decision falls to the Husband. God holds him Accountable for Family Leadership. 1 Corinthians 11: (3) Wives support your Husbands. **God is a God of Order** - The Respect of Order keeps out the Spirit of Rebellion which The Dream Team must show their Submission to God and to each other. When God told Adam, Noah and Abraham, to do something, the Family did not take a Vote! But remember all through the Bible, Women of God brought Men of God, Words From God, Women like Deborah, Abigail, Huldah. **Be Wise Man of God. A Wise Man Esteem Holy Spirit and Word Filled Help, She is your Helpmate, RIGHT!**

8. **The Holy Spirit** - is the **Helper**, **Revealer** and **He, Empowers us**. **He is the Revealer of The Mind of Christ**. The Team needs the Baptism of the Holy Spirit Acts 2:(38). He is our Holy Spirit (Help), along with the Word of God to bring all that Jesus have and knows' in the Mind of Christ, also Power and Ability.

Praying in the Spirit means talking directly from your Spirit to God (Who is a Spirit). With this ability for Spiritual Conversation, the Lord is giving answers to mysteries of your life and even others. (1 Corinthians 14:2) This **Spiritual Conversation Brings Supernatural Faith** to **Believe** what **GOD HAS PROMISED. Jude 1:(20)** The Holy Spirit release's his Power and Ability of Help and Support. Acts 1:(8) and 2 Timothy 1:(6).

When it comes to Unity in your Home, **The Holy Spirit and The Word has no Division of Truth. When a Husband and Wife Submit to the Lords' Helper (i.e. THE HOLY SPIRIT AND GODS' WORD),** it will make it hard for Satan to get a foot hole in God's

Victory Plan. Also checking one of our worse enemy's, the flesh(one wanting his or her own way or being or staying offended). LOVE AND UNITY BRINGS AND KEEPS THE VICTORY BECAUSE *1 CORINTHIANS 13:(4-8)*

(4) Charity (LOVE) suffereth long, and is kind; charity; envieth not; charity vaunteth not itself, is not puffed up, (5) Doth not behave itself unseemly, seeketh not her own, is not easily provoked, thinketh no evil; (6) Rejoiceth not in iniquity, but rejoiceth in the truth;(7) Beareth all things, believeth all things, hopeth all things, endureth all things. (8) Charity *(LOVE)* never Faileth:

OUR VICTORY IS ASSURED BECAUSE OF OUR LORD JESUS CHRIST BY HIS SPIRIT OF LOVE AND UNITY MAKE'S US CONFIDENT IN THIS TRUTH WE HAVE ALREADY WON!

ME AND MY WIFE HAVE SPOKEN OVER THIS WORD FROM GOD, THE BLESSING OF OUR LORD JESUS THE CHRIST FOR YOU AND YOUR FAMILY. LET THERE BE LOVE, ORDER AND UNITY.

YOUR LOVING BROTHER AND SISTER IN CHRIST,

EVANGELIST IVORY AND PHYLLIS HERD

CHAPTER 5

God's Team Order For The Love And Respect For The Success Of The Team

- *(2 Cor. 6:14)* Be ye not unequally yoked together with unbelievers : for what fellowship hath righteousness with unrighteousness: and what communion hath light with darkness?

- *(1 Corn. 11:3)* I would have you know, that the head of every man is Christ: and the head of the woman is the man: and the head of Christ is God.

- *(1 Peter 3:1-7)* Ye wives, be in subjection to your husband's; that, if any obey not the word, they also may without the word be won by the conversation of the wives, while they behold your chaste conversation coupled with fear. Whose adorning let it not be that outward adorning of plaiting the hair, and of wearing of gold, or of putting on a apparel: but let it be the hidden man of the heart, in that which is not corruptible, even the ornament of a meek and quiet spirit, which is in the sight of God of great price. For after this manner in the old time the holy women also, who trusted in God, adorned themselves, being in subjection unto their own husbands: even as Sarah obeyed Abraham calling him lord: whose daughters ye are, as long as ye do well, and are not afraid with any amazement. Likewise, ye husbands , dwell with them according to knowledge, giving honour unto the wife, as unto the weaker vessel, and as being heirs together of the grace of life; that your prayers be not hindered.

- **(Col. 3:18-21)** Wives, submit yourselves unto your own husband, as it is fit in the Lord. Husbands, love your wives, and be not bitter against them. Children, obey your parents in all things: for this is well-pleasing unto the Lord, Fathers, provoke not your children to anger, lest they be discouraged.

- **(1 Tim. 5:8)** If any provide not for his own, and especially for those of his own house, he hath denied the faith, and is worse than an infidel.

- **(Eph. 6:1-4)** Children, obey your parents in the Lord: for this is right. Honor they father and mother; which is the first commandment with promise; that it may be well with thee, and thou mayest live long on the earth. And, ye fathers provoke not your children to wrath: but bring them up in the nurture and admonition of the Lord .

- **(1 Cor. 7:10-15)** Unto the married I command, yet not I, but the Lord, Let not the wife depart from her husband: but if she depart, let her remain unmarried or be reconciled to her husband: and let not the husband and let not the husband put away his wife...And the woman which hath an husband that believeth not, and if he be pleased to dwell with her, let her not leave him. For the unbelieving husband is sanctified by the wife, and unbelieving wife is sanctified by the husband: else were your children unclean; but now are they holy. But if the unbelieving depart, let him depart. A brother or a sister is not under bondage in such cases: but God hath called us to peace

- **(1 Cor. 7:2-5)** Let every man have his own wife, and let every woman have her own husband. Let the husband render unto the wife due benevolence: and likewise also the wife unto the husband: The wife hath not power of her own body, but the husband: and likewise also the husband hath not power of his own body, but the wife. Defraud ye not one the other, except it be with consent for a time, that ye may give yourselves to fasting and prayer; and come together again, that Satan tempt you not for your incontinency.

- **(Ephesians 5:31)** [31] For this cause shall a man leave his father and mother, and shall be joined unto his wife, and they <u>two shall be one flesh.</u>

- **(Matt 18:18-19)** ^{18}Verily I say unto you, Whatsoever ye shall bind on earth shall be bound in heaven: and whatsoever ye shall loose on earth shall be loosed in heaven. ^{19}Again I say unto you, That if <u>two</u> of you shall <u>agree</u> on earth as touching anything that they shall ask, it shall be done for them of my Father which is in heaven.

- **(Psalms 133:1)** Behold, how good and how pleasant it is for brethren to dwell <u>together in unity!</u>

- **(Ecclesiastes 4:9-10)** **(9)** Two are better than one; because they have a good reward for their labour. **(10)** For if they fall, the one will lift up his fellow: but woe to him that is alone when he falleth; for him hath not another to help him up.

(1 Corinthians 11:3) But I would have you know, that the head of every man is Christ; and the head of the woman is the man; and the head of Christ is God.

- **(1 Corinthians 13: 4-8)** (4) Charity **(LOVE)** suffereth long and is kind love envieth not; (5) Doth not behave itself unseemly, seeketh not her own, is not easily provoked, thinketh no evil. (6) Rejoiceth not in iniquity, but rejoiceth in the truth; (7) Beareth all things, hopeth all things, endureth all things. (8) Love never Faileth.

- **(II Timothy 1: 5)** When I called to remembrance the unfeigned faith that is in thee, which dwell first in thy grandmother, Lois, and their mother Eunice, and I am persuaded what is thee also.

- **(Proverbs 14: 1)** Every wise woman buildeth her house: but the foolish plucketh it down with her hands.

Notes:

Ministry Contact Information

Evangelist Ivory & Phyllis Herd

Website:

Ivoryherd.com

Email:

irelyonchrist8@yahoo.com

Telephone Numbers:

Evangelist Ivory Herd
310-971-1157

Sister Phyllis Herd
424-477-8787

www.ingramcontent.com/pod-product-compliance
Lightning Source LLC
Chambersburg PA
CBHW071648040426
42452CB00009B/1806